PIANO PLAY-ALONG
CD INCLUDED

Easy Christmas Melodies
with duet accompaniments

arranged by
Cynthia Pace

T0066100

Contents

CHRISTMAS MELODIES CD recordings provide three "play-along" tracks for each duet as follows: 1) Melody and Accompaniment Parts together - performance tempo, 2) Melody and Accompaniment Parts together - practice tempo, 3) Accompaniment Part - performance tempo.

Lee Roberts Music Publications Inc.
Chatham, New York

DISTRIBUTED BY

HAL•LEONARD CORPORATION
7777 W. BLUEMOUND RD. P.O. BOX 13819 MILWAUKEE, WI 53212

Copyright © 2007 by Cynthia Pace
International Copyright Secured
All Rights Reserved

G Major Tune-up

Key of G Major

Jingle Bells

J. Pierpont

Jin - gle bells,   jin - gle bells,   jin - gle all the way,

Accompaniment Part (Play solo part one octave higher than written):

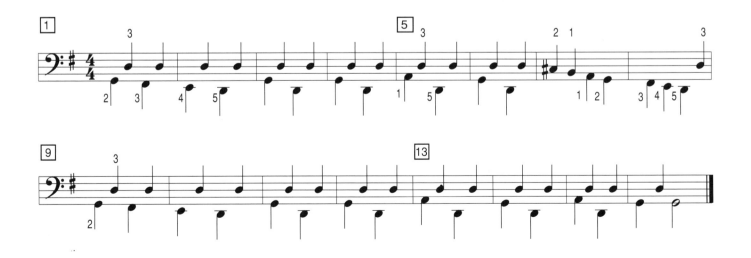

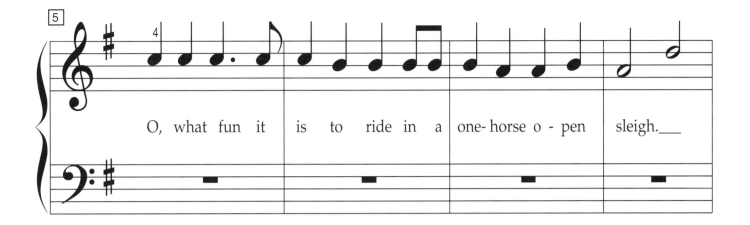

O, what fun it is to ride in a one-horse o-pen sleigh.___

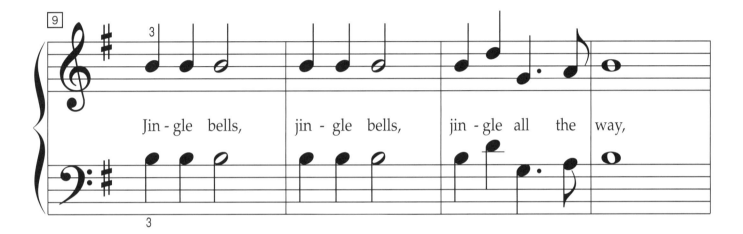

Jin-gle bells, jin-gle bells, jin-gle all the way,

O, what fun it is to ride in a one-horse o-pen sleigh!

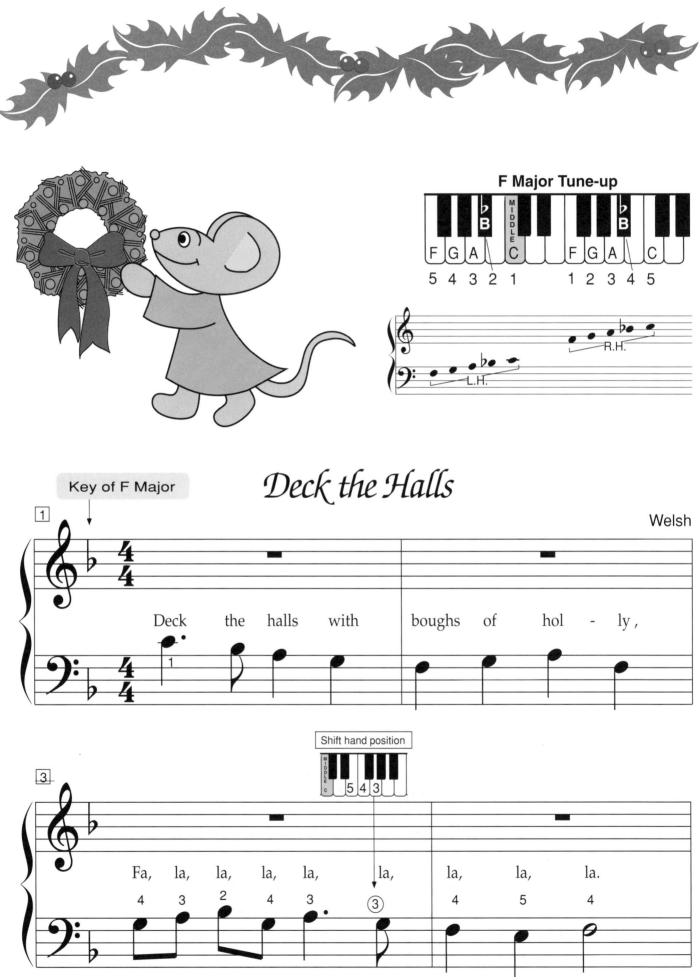

F Major Tune-up

Key of F Major

Deck the Halls

Welsh

Deck the halls with boughs of hol - ly,

Shift hand position

Fa, la, la, la, la, la, la, la, la.

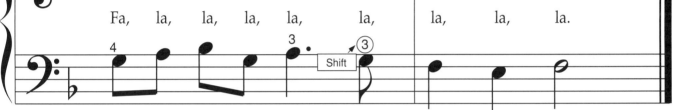

'Tis the sea - son to be jol - ly,

Fa, la, la, la, la, la, la, la, la.

Accompaniment Part (Play solo part one octave higher than written):

We Three Kings

John H. Hopkins

Key of D Minor*

We three kings of O - ri - ent are;

Bear - ing gifts, we trav - erse a - far.

*D minor and F major are RELATIVE KEYS. They share the same key signature.

2424

<u>Accompaniment Part</u> (Play solo part one octave higher than written):

Jolly Old Saint Nicholas

Traditional

Key of G Major

Jol - ly old Saint Nich -o- las, lean your ear this way!

Accompaniment Part (Play above solo part one octave higher than written):

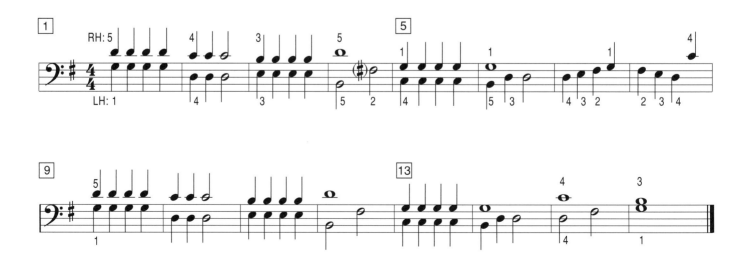

Don't you tell a sin-gle soul what I'm going to say;

Christ-mas Eve is com-ing soon, now you dear old man,

Whis-per what you'll bring to me, tell me if you can.

O Come Little Children

J.A.P. Schulz

Key of F Major

O come lit - tle child - ren, to Beth - le - hem all! Where

Accompaniment Part (Play solo part as written):

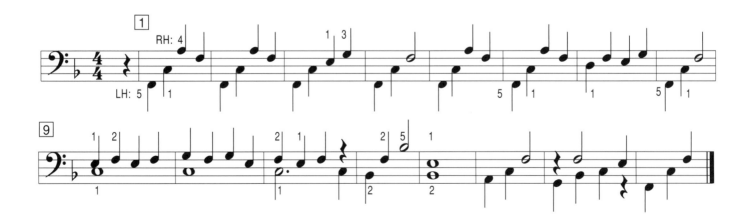

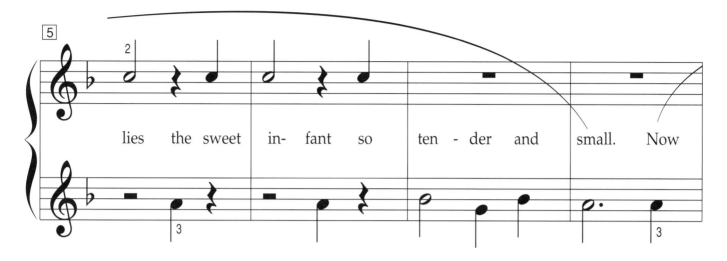

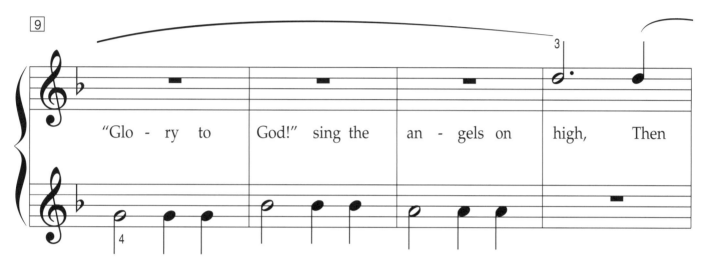

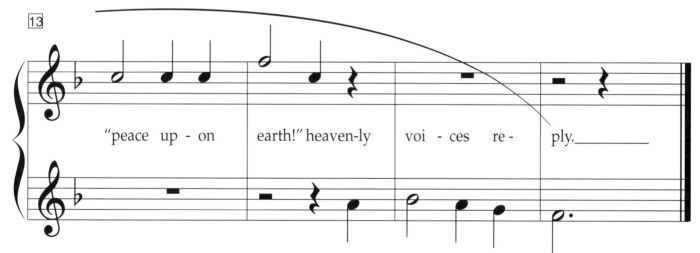

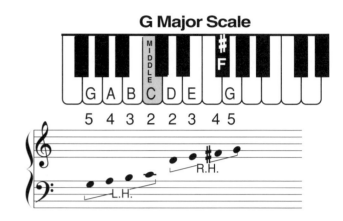

G Major Scale

Key of G Major

The First Noel

French

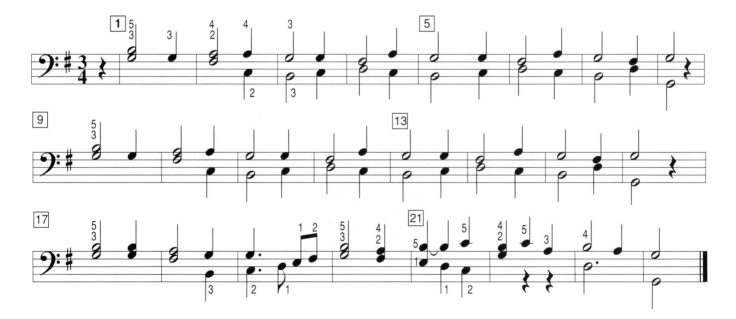

The ___ first _____ No - el, the ___ an - gels did say, Was to

Accompaniment Part (Play solo part one octave higher than written):

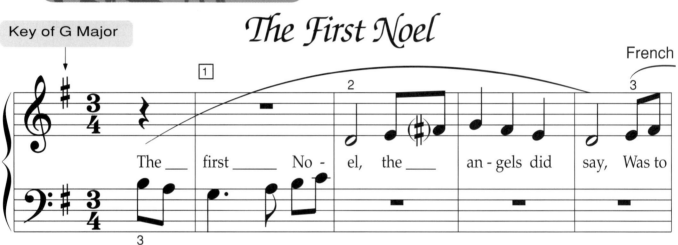

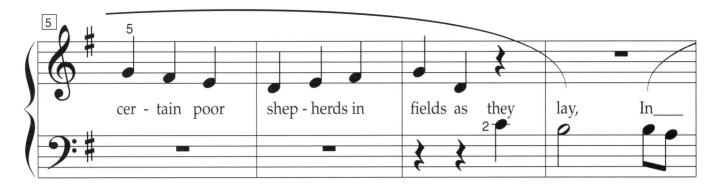

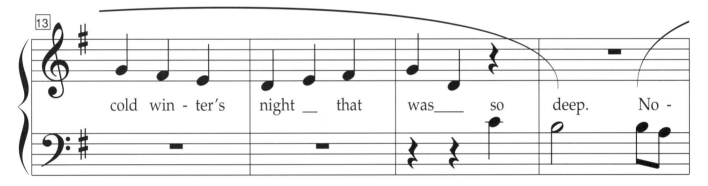

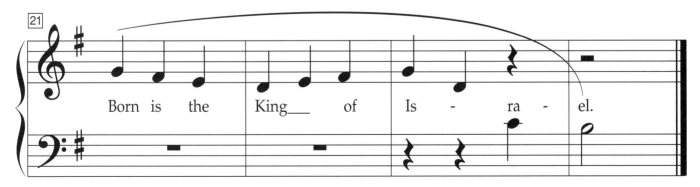

Joy to the World!

G.F. Handel
I. Watts

Key of D Major

Joy to the world! The Lord is come: Let

Accompaniment Part (Play solo part as written):

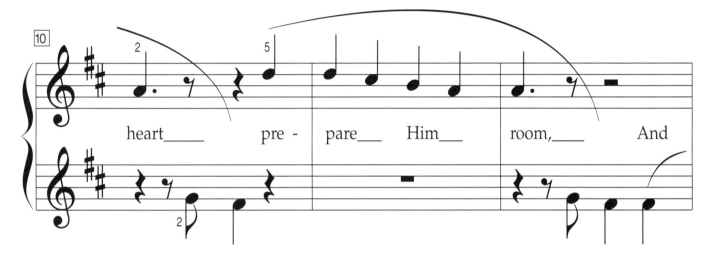

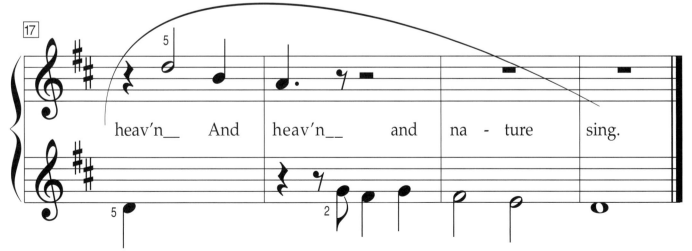

Up On the House-top

B. R. Hanby

Key of F Major

Up   on the house-top the | rein-deer pause, | Out jumps good old

Accompaniment Part (Play solo part one octave higher than written):

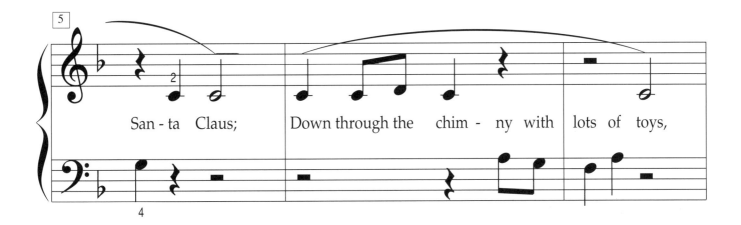

Silent Night

Key of C Major

Franz Gruber
Joseph Mohr

Si - lent night! Ho - ly night! All is

Accompaniment Part (Play solo part one octave higher than written):

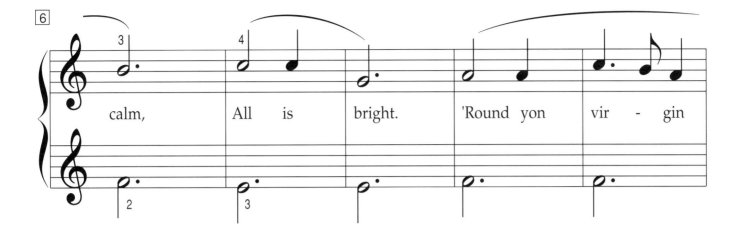

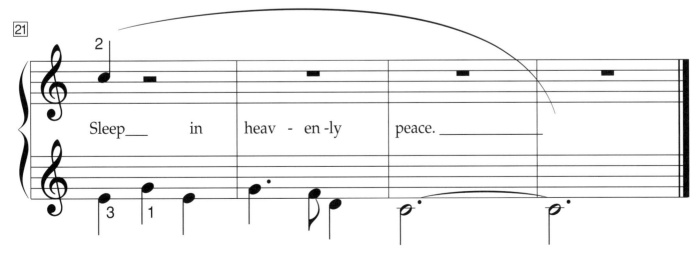

2424

F Major Scale Tones

Angels We Have Heard On High

Key of F Major

French

An-gels we have heard on high, sweet-ly sing-ing o'er the plains.

Accompaniment Part (Play solo part one octave higher than written):

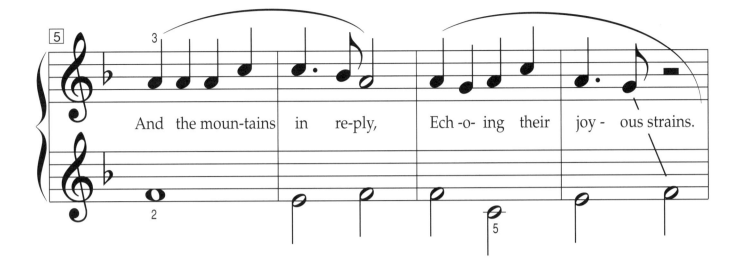

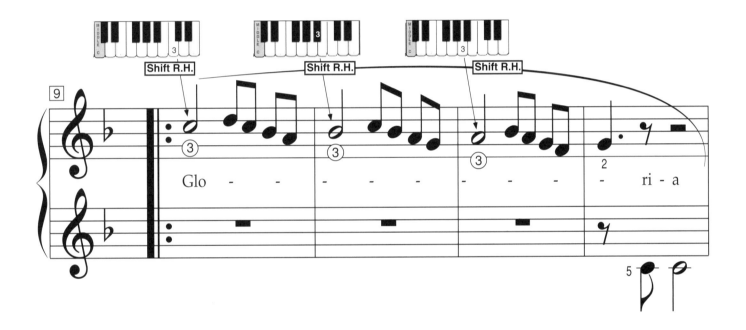

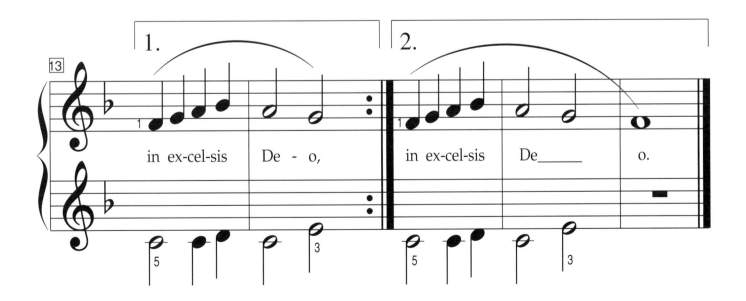

C Major Scale Tones

Go Tell It On The Mountain

swing style

Spiritual

1 Key of C Major

Go tell it on the moun - tain,

Accompaniment Part (Play solo part one octave higher than written):

C Major Scale Tones

We Wish You A Merry Christmas

Key of C Major

English

We wish you a Mer-ry | Christ-mas, we | wish you a Mer-ry | Christ-mas, we

<u>Accompaniment Part</u> (Play solo part one octave higher than written):

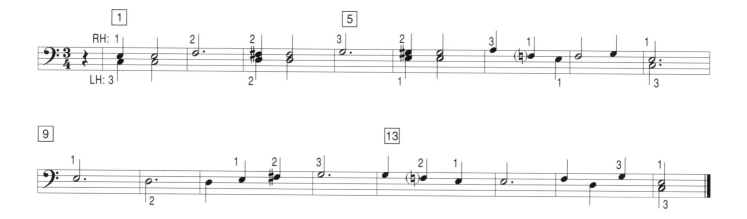

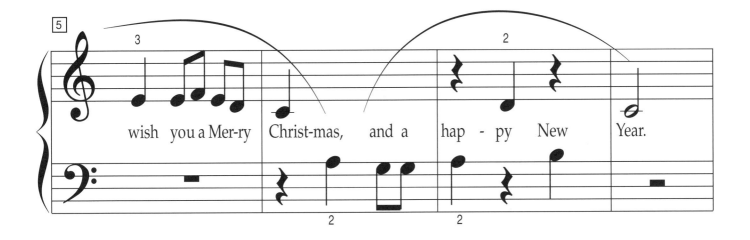

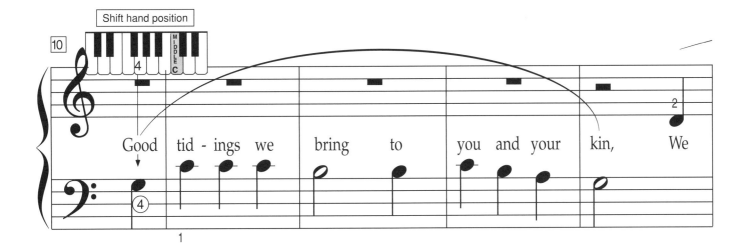

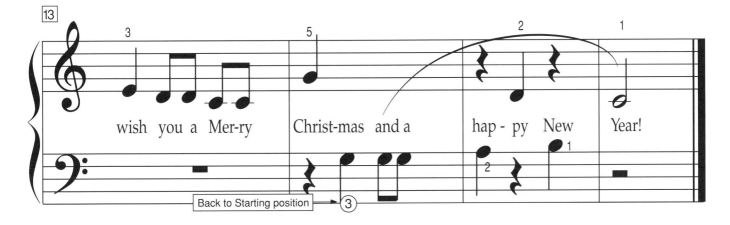

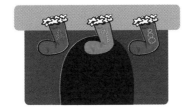

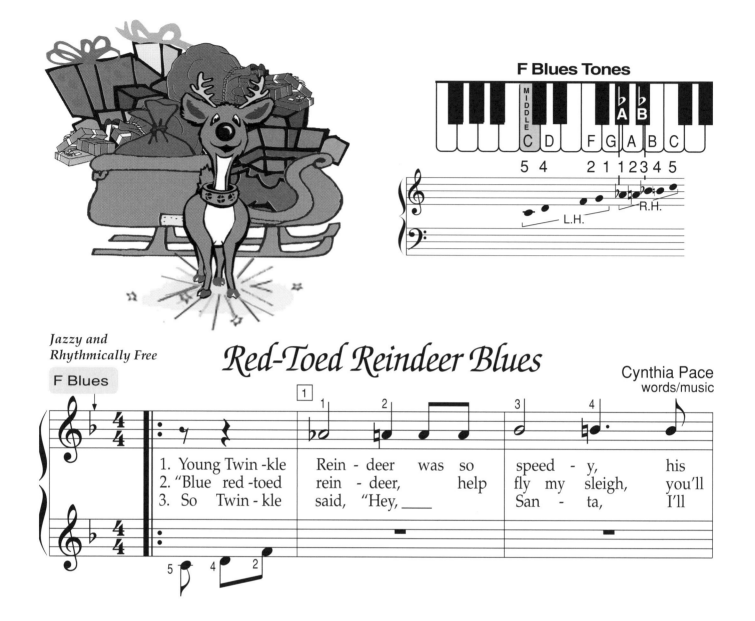

F Blues Tones

Jazzy and Rhythmically Free

Red-Toed Reindeer Blues

Cynthia Pace
words/music

F Blues

1. Young Twin -kle Rein - deer was so speed - y, his
2. "Blue red -toed rein - deer, help fly my sleigh, you'll
3. So Twin - kle said, "Hey, ____ San - ta, I'll

Accompaniment Part (Play accompaniment 1 octave LOWER. Play solo part as written):

(Verse 3: Skip from m. 3 to Coda, pg. 28

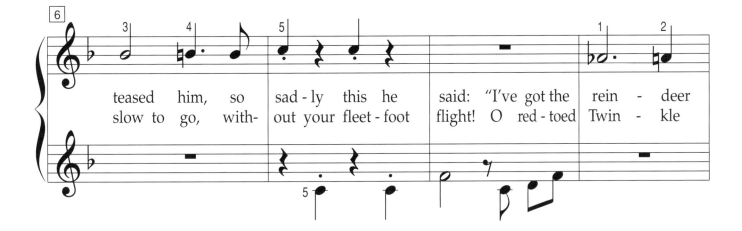

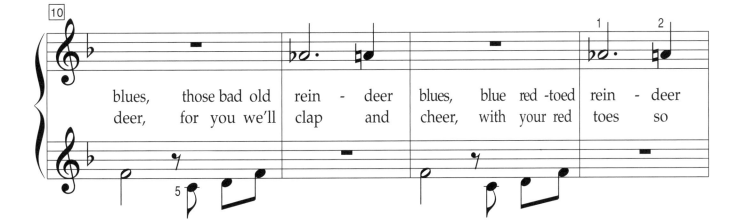

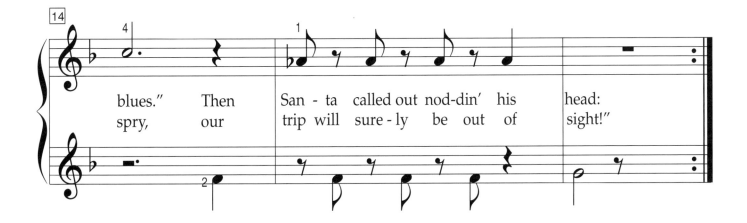

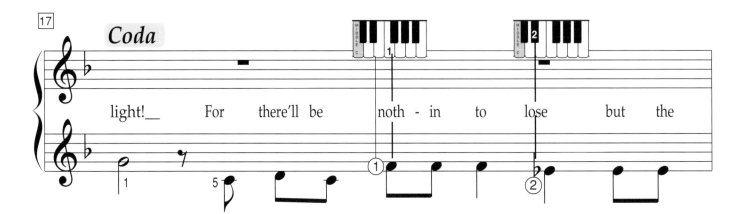

light!__ For there'll be noth - in to lose but the

rein - deer blues, as we glide all thru the sky to - night. Yeah!"

Accompaniment Part (Cont'd.):

Coda